eme R

Undercover
Creatures

By Katharine Kenah

School Specialty
Publishing
Columbus, Ohio

School Specialty
Publishing

Copyright © 2005 School Specialty Publishing, a member of the School
Specialty Family.

Library of Congress Cataloging-in-Publication Data is on file with the publisher.

Send all inquiries to:
School Specialty Publishing
8720 Orion Place
Columbus, OH 43240-2111

ISBN 0-7696-3181-9

3 4 5 6 7 8 9 10 PHX 09 08 07 06 05

Some animals hide
to stay safe from enemies.
They change color.
They change shape.
They have spots.
They have stripes.

Turn the page to see how some
animals hide in the wild.

Polar Bear

Look closely. What do you see?
You see a polar bear and its cub.
They live in a land of ice and snow.
White fur keeps them warm.
It also makes them hard to see.

Stick Insect

Look closely. What do you see?
You see a stick insect.
A small head and a long,
thin body make it hard to see.
It looks like a tree branch.

Gecko

Look closely. What do you see?
You see a gecko.
It uses its toes to climb trees.
Its brown, bumpy skin makes it
hard to see on a log.

Bengal Tiger

Look closely. What do you see?
You see a Bengal tiger.
Each tiger has a different set of stripes.
The stripes make the tiger
hard to see in tall grass.

Leafy Sea Dragon

Look closely. What do you see?
You see a leafy sea dragon.
Its skin grows flaps that look like
waving seaweed.
Hungry fish do not see
the leafy sea dragon.

Peacock Flounder

Look closely. What do you see?
You see a peacock flounder.
It lives in the sand and mud
under the sea.
Its skin changes color
to look like its home.

Bullfrog

Look closely. What do you see?
You see a bullfrog.
Its dark stripes and yellow-green color
look like water and grass.
It hides well in a pond or stream.

Snow Leopard

Look closely. What do you see?
You see a snow leopard.
It lives in high places with lots of snow.
Its pale fur and dark spots make it
hard to see among snow and rocks.

Chameleon

Look closely. What do you see?
You see a chameleon.
It can be brown on the ground.
It can turn green in a tree.
A chameleon can change
its color quickly!

Snowshoe Hare

Look closely. What do you see?
You see a snowshoe hare.
Its fur is brown in the summer
and white in the winter.
The hare's fur helps it hide
from other animals.

Dik-Dik

Look closely. What do you see?
You see a dik-dik.
It is small and quick.
Its brown fur makes it
hard to see in the woods.

Moth

Look closely. What do you see?
You see a moth.
Its wings are hard to see
next to the gray tree bark.
Its wing spots look like eyes.
The spots scare away birds.

Green Snake

Look closely. What do you see?
You see a green snake.
It is covered with small, hard plates
called *scales*.
Green scales are hard to see
in green leaves.

Snail

Look closely. What do you see?
You see a snail.
It lives in wet, dark places.
It looks for plants to eat at night.
Its small shell is hard to see
in a garden.

EXTREME FACTS ABOUT UNDERCOVER CREATURES!

- Polar bears can run at 35 mph for short periods of time. This is faster than human beings can run!

- Unlike most insects, stick insects have no wings.

- If a gecko is attacked, its tail breaks off and still wiggles!

- The roar of the Bengal tiger can be heard two miles away.

- When leafy sea dragons change colors to match their backgrounds, their eyes change colors, too.

- Peacock flounders are shaped like typical fish when they hatch. When they grow to a half-inch long, their bodies flatten and both eyes appear on the same side of their heads.

- Female bullfrogs lay 20,000 eggs at one time.

- Snow leopards cannot roar. They purr like domestic cats.

- Chameleons' tongues shoot out so rapidly that the human eye cannot see them!

- The coats of the snowshoe hare change color with the season, but the tips of their ears are always black.

- Dik-diks are only 14 inches tall at their shoulders, the size of small dogs.

- Moths have been used to make silk in China for over 4,000 years.

- Green snakes never blink! They have no eyelids.

- As snails grow bigger, their shells grow bigger, too.